DREAMS
PLANS
ACHIEVEMENTS

MOVING TOWARDS
YOUR GREATNESS!

Welcome!

It's time to get Moving Towards Your Greatness!

Thank you for taking the time to purchase this powerful book–Moving Towards Your Greatness! Success comes in many forms. It is very important that we pay attention when success shows up!

I pray that this book will help you along your journey to success. God has many blessings in store for us on this journey called life. The key is to make sure we are lining ourselves up with His plans for us. In the book of Jeremiah 29:11 God tells us that He knows the plans He has for us; plans to prosper us and not to harm us, plans to give us hope and a future! This allows us to feel confident in the direction that has been laid out for us. So, as we focus on the plans that God has for us, we must keep our eyes on the prize at all times.

Nora Shariff Borden

Printed in the United States of America
First Printing, 2020

MOVING TOWARDS YOUR GREATNESS!

JANUARY

Message from Nora:

What are you building in January?
I want you to think about what you
are building! Your vision and your
dreams are your foundation for
your building! So ask yourself this
question—what am I building?

Guiding Bible Verse:

"Your gifts will make room for you
and put you before great people."
- Psalms 32:8

JANUARY

SUN	MON	TUE	WED	THU	FRI	SAT

MONTHLY GOALS

"A dream written down with a date becomes a GOAL.
A goal broken down into steps becomes a PLAN. A plan backed
by ACTION makes your dreams come true."

NOTES

Take a moment and list down everything you have on your mind.

FEBRUARY

Message from Nora:

Love and Relationships!

Make sure you are always keeping your love and respect open at all times. You must always be honest and work hard to have trusting relationships! And we must learn to be patient with each other, just as God is patient with us!!

Guiding Bible Verse:

"Above all, love one another deeply, because love covers a multitude of sins."
- 1 Peter 4:8

FEBRUARY

SUN	MON	TUE	WED	THU	FRI	SAT

MONTHLY GOALS

Break your goals down into an Action Plan Checklist.

☐ _____

☐ _____

☐ _____

☐ _____

☐ _____

☐ _____

☐ _____

☐ _____

☐ _____

☐ _____

☐ _____

☐ _____

☐ _____

☐ _____

☐ _____

☐ _____

☐ _____

☐ _____

☐ _____

☐ _____

☐ _____

☐ _____

☐ _____

☐ _____

☐ _____

☐ _____

☐ _____

☐ _____

NOTES

Record everything that grabs your attention.

MARCH

Message from Nora:

Spring is the time to refresh your mind! I Love Spring! It is such a beautiful time of the year. It is a time when we can have a clear perspective of things that we are doing or planning to do. Our minds must be clear when we are planning our future along with God. I love being in partnership with Him because He is the ultimate planner!

Guiding Bible Verse:

"But seek first the kingdom and His righteousness, and all these things will be given to you as well."
- Matthew 6:33

MARCH

SUN	MON	TUE	WED	THU	FRI	SAT

MONTHLY GOALS

"My goal is not to be better than anyone else,
but to be better than I used to be."
- Dwayne D. Dyer

_____

_____

_____

_____

_____

_____

_____

_____

_____

_____

_____

_____

_____

_____

_____

_____

_____

_____

_____

_____

_____

_____

_____

_____

NOTES

Your client meetings, grocery shopping list, that "big idea" you thought of in the subway, your business strategies, the habits you're trying to develop, that quote you liked, the song lyrics you heard, your mother-in-law's birthday.

APRIL

Message from Nora:

Stay strong! If you get tired, learn to rest, not quit! On this journey to our dreams we must learn to rest! Now let me be clear, that does not mean stop and do nothing. No, rest means take a step back, to rest and reflect on what your next move should be! You will find when you do that, things will move a lot faster in your favor!

Guiding Bible Verse:

"Come to me, all you who are weary and burdened, and I will give you rest. Take my yoke upon you and learn from me, for I am gentle and humble in heart, and you will find rest for your souls. For my yoke is easy and my burden is light!"
- Matthew 11:28-30

APRIL

SUN	MON	TUE	WED	THU	FRI	SAT

MONTHLY GOALS

Visualization is the key to making your goals a reality.

_____

_____

_____

_____

_____

_____

_____

_____

_____

_____

_____

_____

_____

_____

_____

_____

_____

_____

_____

_____

_____

_____

_____

_____

_____

_____

_____

NOTES

As David Allen, the author of the best-selling book
"Getting Things Done" suggests, our minds are for having ideas,
not storing them—write it down.

MAY

Message from Nora:

Sometimes we can only find our true direction when we believe in ourselves. It is so important to believe in one's self. It doesn't matter what others say or think about you; the only thing that matters is what you are saying about yourself!

Guiding Bible Verse:

"But these are written so that you may continue to believe that Jesus is the Messiah, the Son of God, and that by believing in Him you have life by the power of His name!"
- John 20:31

MAY

SUN	MON	TUE	WED	THU	FRI	SAT

MONTHLY GOALS

What are you believeing God for - write them down?

_____

_____

_____

_____

_____

_____

_____

_____

_____

_____

_____

_____

_____

_____

_____

_____

_____

_____

_____

_____

_____

_____

NOTES

Writing things down helps clarify your goals, priorities, and intentions.

JUNE

Message from Nora:

Turn lemons into lemonade!

It is so important when life throws you lemons you must immediately turn it into lemonade! This will help you see your situation from a different perspective. When that happens, life looks clearer!

Guiding Bible Verse:

"I have told you these things so that in me you may have peace. In this world you will have trouble. But take heart! I have overcome the world."
- John 16:33

JUNE

SUN	MON	TUE	WED	THU	FRI	SAT

MONTHLY GOALS

"Adversity is preparation for greatness."
- Andy Andrews

_____

_____

_____

_____

_____

_____

_____

_____

_____

_____

_____

_____

_____

_____

_____

_____

_____

_____

_____

_____

_____

_____

_____

_____

_____

NOTES

Writing things down helps keep you inspired about your greatness.

JULY

Message from Nora:

The greatest, cherished moments are when friends and family come together.

There is so much fun, peace, joy, and laughter. It has been said that laughter is good for the soul! Make sure you are making every day a day of laughter!

Guiding Bible Verse:

"Then our mouth was filled with laughter and our tongue with shouts of joy; then they said among the nations, "The Lord has done great things for them."
- Psalms 126:2

JULY

SUN	MON	TUE	WED	THU	FRI	SAT

MONTHLY GOALS

Friends and family gather here.

_____

_____

_____

_____

_____

_____

_____

_____

_____

_____

_____

_____

_____

_____

_____

_____

_____

_____

_____

_____

_____

_____

_____

_____

_____

NOTES

Write down the things you want to do with your family and friends.

AUGUST

Message from Nora:

Take time to plan and reflect every
year on the projects ahead. This
will help you clearly see if the plans
you have put in place are on point!
I suggest you go to a quiet place,
preferably somewhere near the
water, there is such peace there.
And you won't be surprised when
the Lord shows up to meet you
there!

Guiding Bible Verse:

"As in water, the face reflects the
face, So the heart of a man (or
woman) reflects man (or woman)."
- Proverbs 27:19

AUGUST

SUN	MON	TUE	WED	THU	FRI	SAT

MONTHLY GOALS

"The habit of persistence is the habit of victory."
- Herbert Kaufman.

NOTES

By writing things down, you have a record of what you did, thought of, and acted on. This will help you reflect on what worked and what did not.

"Autumn is a second spring where every leaf is a flower."
~Albert Camus

SEPTEMBER

Message from Nora:

Through hard work and perseverance and faith in God you can always live out your dreams.

The key point here is making sure you are allowing your faith in God to help you see your dreams as they become a reality!

Guiding Bible Verse:

"Now faith is the confidence in what we hope for and assurance for what we do not see!"
- Hebrews 11:1

SEPTEMBER

SUN	MON	TUE	WED	THU	FRI	SAT

MONTHLY GOALS

Be fearless in your pursuant of what sets your soul on fire!

NOTES

The key to daily progress is writing is down.

OCTOBER

Message from Nora:

"Striving for success; without hard work is like trying to harvest where you haven't planted." - David Bly

It is reassuring that when you work to achieve your dreams, success will show up! For God promises to bless the work of our hands.

Guiding Bible Verse:

"The Lord will open the heavens, the storehouse of his bounty, to send rain on your land in season and to bless all the work of your hands. You will lend to many nations but will borrow from none."
- Deuteronomy 28:12

OCTOBER

SUN	MON	TUE	WED	THU	FRI	SAT

MONTHLY GOALS

*"And the sun took a step back, and the leaves lulled themselves to sleep
and autumn was awakened." - Raquel Franco
It's time to wake up your dreams.*

_____

_____

_____

_____

_____

_____

_____

_____

_____

_____

_____

_____

_____

_____

_____

_____

_____

_____

_____

_____

_____

_____

_____

_____

_____

_____

_____

NOTES

"Always carry a notebook. Write everything down...that is a million-dollar lesson they don't teach you in business school!"
- Aristotle Onassis

NOVEMBER

Message from Nora:

November is the month for us to be reminded to be thankful for the many blessings that God has sent our way. As we reflect on these many blessings, let us be mindful of how important it is to give. When we give with the right motive; we can be reassured of the blessings of the Lord.

Guiding Bible Verse:

"You will be enriched in every way so that you can be generous on every occasion, and through us your generosity will result in thanksgiving to God!"
- 2 Corinthians 9:11

NOVEMBER

SUN	MON	TUE	WED	THU	FRI	SAT

MONTHLY GOALS

There's always something to be thankful for—write it down.

NOTES

Writing things down enables a higher level of thinking,
and therefore, more focused action.

DECEMBER

Message from Nora:

May this month bring you warmth, love, smiles, and everything that fills your heart with the peace that this time of the year brings.

It is so important that we remember that Jesus is the reason for this season! God bless you!

Guiding Bible Verse:

"And she shall bring forth a son, and thou shall call his name Jesus: for He shall save His people from their sins!"
- Matthew 1:21

DECEMBER

SUN	MON	TUE	WED	THU	FRI	SAT

MONTHLY GOALS

This is the month to reflect on all that you have
accomplished throughout the year.

_____

_____

_____

_____

_____

_____

_____

_____

_____

_____

_____

_____

_____

_____

_____

_____

_____

_____

_____

_____

_____

_____

_____

_____

_____

_____

_____

NOTES

Writing things down can help our brains prioritize which things we should focus on and act on, at any given moment.

FAITH

PRODUCTIVITY

HEALTH

FINANCES

LOVE

POWER

FOCUS

SCHEDULE

FAMILY

FUN

LEARNING

GIVE BACK

FAITH

Bible Study

Belief

Prayer Life

Be Still

Meditate

PRODUCTIVITY

Apps

Time Schedule

Breaks

Breath

Plan

HEALTH

Meal Prep

Recipes

Eliminate Sugar

Exercise

Walking

Sleep

Vacation

Self Care

FINANCES

Spending Plan

Pay Down Debt

Raise Credit Score

Hire Tax Expert

Savings

Start a Business

LOVE

Family

Relationships

Self Confidence

Self-Love

Complimenting Others

POWER

Strength

Be Bold

Act

Do

FOCUS

Plan

Prepare

Set Goals

Write

SCHEDULE

Journaling

Bible Study

Learning

Dates

Time with Children

Friends

Vacation

Rest

FAMILY

Game Night

Dinners

Cookouts

Vacations

Gatherings

Communication

FUN

Vacation

Movies

Music

Get Active

Connecting

Adventurous

LEARNING

Reading Plan

Online Classes

New Skills

Hobbies

GIVE BACK

Volunteer

Time

NOTES

What are you thinking about?

NOTES

Out of your head. Write it down.

NOTES

Put pen to paper.

NOTES

Capture your thoughts.

NOTES

Ideas are powerful.

NOTES

Write down an idea, and your subconscious will reward you with a hundred new ones.

NOTES

Writing things down saves mental energy.

NOTES

Writing is more evident than thoughts.

NOTES

It makes you more committed.

NOTES

Writing your thoughts and ideas down, helps you to think big!

NOTES

You gain a sense of achievement when you write things down.

NOTES

Writing things down can help our brains prioritize what we should focus on and act on at any given moment.

READERS ARE LEADERS

What are you reading this year?

1. *The Bible*
2. *From a Black Man's Perspective* by Nora Shariff Borden
3. *Greatness Awaits You! Journal* by Nora Shariff Borden
4. *Why Are You Sitting on Your Greatness?* by Nora Shariff Borden
5. *You Have the Power to Be Great!* by Nora Shariff Borden
6. *Women Excited in the Word* by Nora Shariff Borden
7. *Affirmation* Cards by Nora Shariff Borden
8. *A Time to Advance* by Chuck D. Pierce
9. *10-Day Green Smoothie Cleanse* by JJ Smith
10. *Green Smoothies for Life* by JJ Smith
11. *Switch on Your Brain: The Key to Peak, Happiness, Thinking, and Health* by Dr. Caroline Leaf
12. *No Ordinary Moments—A Peaceful Warrior's Guide to Daily Life* by Dan Millman
13. *The Battlefield of the Mind* by Joyce Meyer
14. *The Confident Woman* by Joyce Meyer
15. *The Battle Plan for Prayer* by Stephen & Alex Kendrick
16. *Commanding Your Morning—Unleash the Power of God in Your Life* by Cindy Trimm
17. *The Miracle Morning* by Hal Elrod
18. *The Magic of Thinking Big* by Daniel J. Schwartz, Ph.D.
19. *Dream It! Pin It! Live It! Making Vision Boards Work for You* By Terri Savelle Foy
20. *365 Day Brightness—Whispered Words of Encouragement* by Dayspring
21. *A Woman with a Man Behind Her* by Dan Madson
22. *Ask and It is Given* by Esther and Jerry Hicks
23. *He Speaks I Listen* by Michelle McKinney Hammond
24. *The Enemy Called Average* by John Mason

Add your own book list:

25. _____

26. _____

27. _____

28. _____

29. _____

30. _____

31. _____

32. _____

33. _____

34. _____

35. _____

36. _____

37. _____

38. _____

39. _____

40. _____

41. _____

42. _____

43. _____

44. _____

45. _____

46. _____

47. _____

48. _____

49. _____

50. _____

CONTACTS

Name _____ Cell Phone _____

Business Name/Focus _____

Address _____

City _____ St. _____ Zip _____

Email _____

Website _____

_____

Name _____ Cell Phone _____

Business Name/Focus _____

Address _____

City _____ St. _____ Zip _____

Email _____

Website _____

_____

Name _____ Cell Phone _____

Business Name/Focus _____

Address _____

City _____ St. _____ Zip _____

Email _____

Website _____

_____

Name _____ Cell Phone _____

Business Name/Focus _____

Address _____

City _____ St. _____ Zip _____

Email _____

Website _____

CONTACTS

Name _____ Cell Phone _____

Business Name/Focus _____

Address _____

City _____ St. _____ Zip _____

Email _____

Website _____

_____

Name _____ Cell Phone _____

Business Name/Focus _____

Address _____

City _____ St. _____ Zip _____

Email _____

Website _____

_____

Name _____ Cell Phone _____

Business Name/Focus _____

Address _____

City _____ St. _____ Zip _____

Email _____

Website _____

_____

Name _____ Cell Phone _____

Business Name/Focus _____

Address _____

City _____ St. _____ Zip _____

Email _____

Website _____

CONTACTS

Name _____ Cell Phone _____

Business Name/Focus _____

Address _____

City _____ St. _____ Zip _____

Email _____

Website _____

_____

Name _____ Cell Phone _____

Business Name/Focus _____

Address _____

City _____ St. _____ Zip _____

Email _____

Website _____

_____

Name _____ Cell Phone _____

Business Name/Focus _____

Address _____

City _____ St. _____ Zip _____

Email _____

Website _____

_____

Name _____ Cell Phone _____

Business Name/Focus _____

Address _____

City _____ St. _____ Zip _____

Email _____

Website _____

CONTACTS

Name _____ Cell Phone _____

Business Name/Focus _____

Address _____

City _____ St. _____ Zip _____

Email _____

Website _____
_____

Name _____ Cell Phone _____

Business Name/Focus _____

Address _____

City _____ St. _____ Zip _____

Email _____

Website _____
_____

Name _____ Cell Phone _____

Business Name/Focus _____

Address _____

City _____ St. _____ Zip _____

Email _____

Website _____
_____

Name _____ Cell Phone _____

Business Name/Focus _____

Address _____

City _____ St. _____ Zip _____

Email _____

Website _____

BUSINESS RESOURCES

Contact Name	Business Name	Website
Nora Shariff Borden	Business Women on the Move for God (470) 553-4107 info@bwotmfg.com	www.bwotmfg.com
	ACCOUNTANT	
	TAX PREPARER	

BUSINESS RESOURCES

Contact Name	Business Name	Website

FOUNDATIONAL QUOTES

Today is the first day of the rest of your life.

Make each day your masterpiece.
- John Wooden

Love yourself and the rest will follow.

*The secret of change is to focus all of your energy not on fighting the old,
but on building the new.*
- Socrates

*By writing things down, you have a record of what you did, thought of, and acted
on so this helps you reflect on what worked and what didn't.*

*When your brain isn't busy remembering everything,
your brain can then process anything.*

*Think like a queen. A queen is not afraid to fail.
Failure is another steppingstone to greatness.*
- Oprah Winfrey

Greatness is inside all of us, however, first we must choose to be great.

Greatness comes from the desire to do extraordinary things.

*Do not limit yourself. Many people limit themselves to what they
think they can do. You can go as far as your mind lets you.
What you believe, remember you can achieve.*
- Mary Kay Ash

A woman's greatness is all she needs to hold onto when opposition shows up.
- Nora Shariff -Borden

Great things happen when you believe they can.
- Nora Shariff-Borden

*If you are walking down the right path and you're willing to keep walking,
eventually you'll make progress.*
- President Barack Obama

I pray that this book has been a blessing to you, as you travel on your journey to success.

Remember all that you have learned over this year. Focus on looking forward to success and not looking back at your failures. Failures are only there to teach you what not to do, as you move forward, to making your journey lighter and your next steps even greater!

Decide today that you will be all that God has called you to be!

Blessings,

Nora Shariff Borden

12 BLESSED TRUTHS TO YOUR GREATNESS

1. Love yourself. Effect change within your heart and soul in order to be the best person you can be.

2. The Bible says, "Whatever state I am, therewith to be content. You are blessed." Recognize and acknowledge that fact and be happy about being blessed.

3. Relish your solitude and quiet time; do not feel guilty about it because your body and spirit crave it.

4. Be of a giving nature. The Bible says, "Give, and it shall be given unto you." Be willing to give to others and it will be given to you .

5. Learn to forgive yourself and others; letting go of blame frees you to discover the true blessings in your life.

6. Keep it simple: do unto others as you would have them do unto you.

7. Don't strive for perfection; it is not possible. Instead, strive for excellence; it will allow you to operate at your best.

8. Simplify your life by vowing to stop turning minor upsets into major blowups. It will bring down the curtain on drama.

9. Taking care of yourself does not make you self-centered. It makes you centered.

10. Remember; no Jesus, no peace.

11. You must decide to be great, because greatness will never wait on you.

12. Our Greatness is our greatest asset.

WAYS TO CHANGE YOUR THOUGHTS

- You can choose to be poor or prosperous; it is a state of mind.
- The change starts in your mind. It is simple to change the way you think. It is a personal choice.
- Now is the time to choose to change your life, do it now, don't wait.
- Fear and uncertainty deserve no place in your mind.
- Change is necessary.
- To get someplace you've never been or to be someone you've never been, you must do something you've never done.
- What you allow between your left and right ear will determine your thoughts.
- Decide to change and don't get caught in negative thoughts.
- If you get caught up in a step-by-step plan, you're going to find yourself worrying about potential roadblocks that you will encounter, and when you allow that to happen, it leads to fear and uncertainties
- For every problem you encounter, there are at least ten solutions.
- You have the power to change your thoughts.
- Your thoughts become habitual thinking.
- Life is a self-fulfilling prophecy. We get what we expect!
- Whether you think you can or whether you think you can't, you are right either way
- 90% of the outside data that feeds into your conscious mind every day is negative, and fear feeds on that.
- We move in the direction of our dominant thoughts.
- Don't get caught up in the "How To."
- Decide first, and then solve the problem.
- Once you decide to change, all kinds of doors will open for you if you don't give up.
- You must take action to change to get what you want.